Dream Big, Fly High, Reach For The Stars

Published By
Black Royalty Success Publishing
6080 Center Drive Suite 600 unit 232
Los Angeles Ca.90045

Lewis J Citizen

Copyright © 2023

Paperback: ISBN: 978-8294-01913-7

Dream Big, Fly High, Reach For The Stars

DEDICATION

My passion for children books and inspiration for writing them is my third child, Joell, he inspired me to write books for children and individuals with autism.

Dedicated to my son Joell Russell Royalty who has inspired me to follow through with writing books for children. When my son turned three, and a half years old we found out that he has autism and tongue tie. I have been working on children's books and educational videos since he was born to help with his educational learning skills. He has been by my side from the start and finish. I just want to thank him and say I 'm proud of him for being so smart and intelligent without being able to talk or express himself how he want really too.

Dream Big, Fly High, Reach For The Stars

ACKNOWLEDGMENTS

Special Thanks! To my wife, three kids, family members, friends, and love one's that are no longer with us on earth. Thank you all for inspiring me to be the best I can be. Thanks for all the love, support, and help. Thanks for inspiring me on a daily basis, to Dream big, Fly High, and Reach for the Stars, Love always yours truly!

Dream Big, Fly High, Reach For The Stars

Reach for the stars! Keep on believing in your goals and dreams even though they may seem to be taking a long time to come true. Opportunities do come knocking on the door when you least expect them to. Keep hoping for the best things in life.

Dream Big, Fly High, Reach For The Stars

Dream Big, Fly High, Reach For The Stars

When the world makes you feel sad, you can always count on your dreams,if you truly believe in them, they will surely come true. Sometimes life may seem unfair when opportunities don't come knocking on the door when we expect them to. If this happens, one of the best options you may have is to get up, get out, and do something that you love to do. There's always a second opportunity waiting around the corner if you take the time to keep looking for it.

Dream Big, Fly High, Reach For The Stars

Dream Big, Fly High, Reach For The Stars

Don't stop dreaming big because you failed at your first try. Everyone makes mistakes, so keep on flying high, keep on climbing to the top of the hill. Reach for the stars to believe in yourself, and your dreams will come true.

Dream Big, Fly High, Reach For The Stars

Dream Big, Fly High, Reach For The Stars

Dream big, fly high, reach for the stars. I'll be there for you if you be there for me if we are there for each other, there's nothing in this world that we can't do or be. Reach for the stars! Love the extraordinary person you are. Keep on climbing the ladder of success until you reach the top.

Dream Big, Fly High, Reach For The Stars

Dream Big, Fly High, Reach For The Stars

When you dream big, fly high, and reach for the stars, it makes no difference who you are whatever your heart desires will come to you.Dream big! Anything is possible to those who believe in the beauty of dreams. Fly high, and let your true colors shine brightly over you, let your true colors shine bright as the beautiful colors of a rainbow. Dream big fly high as a bird rise higher than a kite never, be afraid to let the light inside of you glow.

Dream Big, Fly High, Reach For The Stars

You can even make a small commitment with yourself by saying something like you will do your best to make your dreams come true would be okay to say. Making an honest bond with yourself towards accomplishing your goals could make a massive difference in how you motivate yourself.

Dream Big, Fly High, Reach For The Stars

Dream Big, Fly High, Reach For The Stars

Dream Big, Fly High, Reach For The Stars

Dream Big, Fly High, Reach For The Stars

Reach for the stars, never be a quitter put on your thinking cap, and keep up the excellent work. Never give up on yourself; Keep on dreaming that you can achieve your goals. The sky is the limit! No one knows what tomorrow holds so, reach for the stars.
Keep climbing higher and higher reach for the stars.
Keep on moving forward on the road of achievement towards a successful future.

Dream Big, Fly High, Reach For The Stars

Dream Big, Fly High, Reach For The Stars

Reach for the stars! Climb every hill climb every mountain in your way. Reach! Climb up every ladder towards success. Reach! Reach for the moon, and you will still be amongst the stars. Reach! Reach out to every opportunity given. There isn't anything stopping you but yourself. Taking care of responsibility respecting other people, along with helping and supporting family members and friends, can take you far, places in life.

Dream Big, Fly High, Reach For The Stars

Dream Big, Fly High, Reach For The Stars

SCHOOL

Dream Big, Fly High, Reach For The Stars

Nothing is impossible to achieve or do if you try hard enough. You can be a doctor, nurse, teacher, police officer, firefighter, sports player, actor, musician, singer, or lawyer. You can even become the president of the United States of America if you work hard enough. Yet the word impossible says I'm possible if you look at it in the right way.

Dream Big, Fly High, Reach For The Stars

Dream Big, Fly High, Reach For The Stars

Dream Big, Fly High, Reach For The Stars

Dream Big, Fly High, Reach For The Stars

Please share some of your happiness, joy, and laughter with a family member or friend that may need a smile to brighten up their day. A few kind words can go a long way, and a few generous actions can help in many ways when someone is feeling sad and blue. Volunteering to help others whenever you can without wanting nothing but a thank you in return is a perfect example of how to share some of your kindness. If you dare to reach for the stars, it can lead to bigger things in life, like sending aircraft into space and exploring the universe and the solar system.

Dream Big, Fly High, Reach For The Stars

Dream Big, Fly High, Reach For The Stars

Fly high! Reach for the stars boys and girls; you never know what you can do till you try. Keep on dreaming big, never underestimate the power of your talents. Keep on seeking to beat the odds without giving up. Growth comes from spreading your wings flying high. So take a deep breath and try again your dreams do not have an expiration date. If you make a mistake the first time around, don't worry because you can always start over and try again. Keep reaching for the stars. Keep dreaming big flying high. Yes! You can do anything that you focus your mind on doing. Never give up on yourself, and never give up on your goals. Dream Big, fly high, reach for the stars.

Dream Big, Fly High, Reach For The Stars

Dream Big, Fly High, Reach For The Stars

Dream Big, Fly High, Reach For The Stars

Dream Big, Fly High, Reach For The Stars

ABOUT THE AUTHOR